50 Samurai Cooking in Japan Recipes

By: Kelly Johnson

Table of Contents

- Miso-Grilled Fish
- Samurai Rice Porridge (Okayu)
- Charcoal-Grilled Eel (Unagi no Kabayaki)
- Tataki (Lightly Seared Fish or Meat)
- Hōtō Noodles (Samurai Miso Stew)
- Wild Boar Hot Pot (Shishi Nabe)
- Samurai Miso Soup with Root Vegetables
- Hand-Pounded Rice Cakes (Mochi)
- Dried Persimmon Snacks (Hoshigaki)
- Soba Noodles with Wild Vegetables
- Grilled River Fish (Ayu no Shioyaki)
- Smoked Duck with Sansho Pepper
- Roasted Chestnuts (Yaki Guri)
- Fermented Rice Bran Pickles (Nukazuke)
- Wild Yam Soup (Jinenjo Jiru)
- Roasted Sweet Potatoes (Yaki Imo)
- Bamboo Shoot and Miso Stir-Fry
- Samurai Tea-Pickled Plums (Umeboshi)
- Grilled Venison with Salt and Miso
- Charred Rice Balls (Yaki Onigiri)
- Samurai-Style Fermented Soybeans (Natto)
- Wild Mushroom and Tofu Soup
- Smoked Fish with Wasabi Leaves
- Samurai Hot Pot with Mountain Herbs
- Salted and Dried Fish (Himono)
- Burdock Root and Carrot Stir-Fry (Kinpira Gobo)
- Samurai Roasted Barley Tea (Mugicha)
- Rice with Chestnuts (Kuri Gohan)
- Fire-Grilled Wild Duck (Kamo Yaki)
- Homemade Soy Sauce Pickles
- Sake-Marinated Salmon (Saikyo Yaki)
- Dried Tofu (Koya Dofu) in Miso Broth
- Wild Greens and Sesame Dressing (Gomaae)
- Fermented Radish and Daikon Salad
- Boiled Lotus Root with Miso Glaze

- Lightly Salted Cucumber and Wakame Salad
- Grilled Tofu with Miso Sauce
- Samurai-Style Herbal Tea Blend
- Barley Rice with Mountain Vegetables
- Wild Ginger Rice Porridge
- Dried Squid with Vinegar and Miso
- Soy Sauce-Braised Bamboo Shoots
- Hand-Pulled Udon Noodles
- Mountain Yam Grated Over Rice (Tororo Gohan)
- Black Sesame Rice Balls
- Wild Mushroom and Wild Rice Pilaf
- Soba Noodles in Hot Dashi Broth
- Slow-Simmered Wild Boar and Root Vegetables
- Samurai Green Tea Rice (Ochazuke)
- Fire-Grilled Salmon with Yuzu Citrus

Miso-Grilled Fish

Ingredients:

- 2 fillets of white fish (cod, sea bass, or snapper)
- 3 tbsp miso paste
- 1 tbsp mirin
- 1 tbsp sake
- 1 tsp sugar
- 1 tbsp soy sauce
- 1 tsp grated ginger

Instructions:

1. Mix miso, mirin, sake, sugar, soy sauce, and ginger into a marinade.
2. Coat fish with the marinade and let it sit for at least 1 hour.
3. Preheat a grill and cook the fish for 3-4 minutes per side until caramelized.
4. Serve hot with rice and pickled vegetables.

Samurai Rice Porridge (Okayu)

Ingredients:

- ½ cup short-grain rice
- 3 cups water or dashi stock
- Salt to taste
- Optional toppings: green onions, umeboshi (pickled plum), nori, sesame seeds

Instructions:

1. Rinse the rice and place it in a pot with water or dashi.
2. Bring to a boil, then lower the heat and simmer for 30-40 minutes.
3. Stir occasionally until the rice becomes soft and porridge-like.
4. Season with salt and add toppings as desired.

Charcoal-Grilled Eel (Unagi no Kabayaki)

Ingredients:

- 2 eel fillets (fresh or frozen)
- 3 tbsp soy sauce
- 2 tbsp mirin
- 1 tbsp sake
- 1 tbsp sugar

Instructions:

1. Mix soy sauce, mirin, sake, and sugar into a sauce.
2. Grill eel over charcoal, brushing it with sauce every few minutes.
3. Cook until glazed and slightly crispy on the edges.
4. Serve over rice with extra sauce.

Tataki (Lightly Seared Fish or Meat)

Ingredients:

- 1 tuna steak or beef sirloin
- 1 tbsp soy sauce
- 1 tbsp mirin
- 1 tsp grated ginger
- 1 tbsp sesame oil
- Green onions and sesame seeds for garnish

Instructions:

1. Heat a pan or grill over high heat.
2. Sear the fish or meat for about 30 seconds per side.
3. Slice thinly and drizzle with soy sauce, mirin, and ginger.
4. Garnish with green onions and sesame seeds.

Hōtō Noodles (Samurai Miso Stew)

Ingredients:

- 200g thick wheat noodles
- 4 cups dashi broth
- 2 tbsp miso paste
- 1 carrot, sliced
- ½ daikon radish, chopped
- 100g pumpkin, diced
- 1 block tofu, cubed

Instructions:

1. Cook noodles in boiling water, then drain.
2. Simmer dashi broth with carrots, radish, and pumpkin for 15 minutes.
3. Stir in miso paste and tofu.
4. Add noodles and serve hot.

Wild Boar Hot Pot (Shishi Nabe)

Ingredients:

- 300g wild boar meat, thinly sliced
- 4 cups dashi broth
- 1 tbsp miso paste
- 1 tbsp soy sauce
- ½ cabbage, chopped
- 1 block tofu, sliced
- 1 green onion, chopped

Instructions:

1. Heat dashi broth and add miso and soy sauce.
2. Add cabbage, tofu, and wild boar meat.
3. Simmer for 15 minutes until tender.
4. Garnish with green onions and serve hot.

Samurai Miso Soup with Root Vegetables

Ingredients:

- 4 cups dashi broth
- 2 tbsp miso paste
- 1 small carrot, sliced
- ½ daikon radish, chopped
- 1 block tofu, cubed
- 1 green onion, chopped

Instructions:

1. Simmer dashi broth with carrot and daikon for 10 minutes.
2. Stir in miso paste until dissolved.
3. Add tofu and green onions.
4. Serve warm with rice.

Hand-Pounded Rice Cakes (Mochi)

Ingredients:

- 2 cups glutinous rice
- 1 cup water
- Cornstarch for dusting

Instructions:

1. Soak rice overnight, then steam until soft.
2. Pound rice in a large mortar until sticky.
3. Shape into small cakes and dust with cornstarch.
4. Serve plain or with sweet red bean paste.

Dried Persimmon Snacks (Hoshigaki)

Ingredients:

- 6 persimmons, peeled
- String for hanging

Instructions:

1. Tie string around persimmons and hang them in a dry place.
2. Massage them daily for 4-6 weeks until soft and wrinkled.
3. Store in an airtight container and enjoy as a sweet treat.

Soba Noodles with Wild Vegetables

Ingredients:

- 200g soba noodles
- 4 cups dashi broth
- 1 tbsp soy sauce
- 1 tbsp mirin
- 100g wild greens (fiddleheads, ramps, or mustard greens)

Instructions:

1. Boil soba noodles, then drain and rinse.
2. Simmer dashi broth with soy sauce and mirin.
3. Add wild greens and cook for 2 minutes.
4. Serve over noodles.

Grilled River Fish (Ayu no Shioyaki)

Ingredients:

- 2 whole ayu (or trout)
- 1 tbsp sea salt
- 1 lemon, sliced

Instructions:

1. Rub fish with salt and let sit for 10 minutes.
2. Grill over an open flame or broiler for 5 minutes per side.
3. Serve with lemon slices.

Smoked Duck with Sansho Pepper

Ingredients:

- 1 duck breast
- 1 tsp salt
- 1 tsp sansho pepper (Japanese pepper)
- 1 tbsp sake
- 1 tbsp soy sauce
- Cherry wood chips for smoking

Instructions:

1. Score the duck breast skin and season with salt and sansho pepper.
2. Heat a pan over medium heat and sear the skin side until crispy, about 5 minutes.
3. Flip and cook for another 2 minutes.
4. Smoke the duck over cherry wood chips in a covered pan or smoker for 10-15 minutes.
5. Let rest before slicing and serving with soy sauce and sake glaze.

Roasted Chestnuts (Yaki Guri)

Ingredients:

- 500g fresh chestnuts
- Water for soaking

Instructions:

1. Score an "X" on each chestnut shell to prevent bursting.
2. Soak in water for 30 minutes.
3. Roast in a pan or oven at 200°C (400°F) for 20-25 minutes, shaking occasionally.
4. Peel and enjoy warm.

Fermented Rice Bran Pickles (Nukazuke)

Ingredients:

- 4 cups rice bran (nuka)
- 4 cups water
- 1 tbsp salt
- 1 tbsp miso (optional)
- 1 piece kombu (dried kelp)
- 1 clove garlic, smashed
- 1 carrot, sliced
- 1 cucumber, sliced

Instructions:

1. Mix rice bran, water, salt, miso, and kombu in a container.
2. Add garlic and vegetables.
3. Submerge vegetables completely and ferment at room temperature for 3-7 days.
4. Rinse before eating.

Wild Yam Soup (Jinenjo Jiru)

Ingredients:

- 1 small wild yam (jinenjo)
- 4 cups dashi broth
- 1 tbsp miso paste
- 1 tbsp soy sauce
- 1 green onion, chopped

Instructions:

1. Peel and grate the wild yam into a sticky paste.
2. Heat dashi broth and dissolve miso paste.
3. Stir in soy sauce and wild yam.
4. Serve with green onions on top.

Roasted Sweet Potatoes (Yaki Imo)

Ingredients:

- 2 Japanese sweet potatoes

Instructions:

1. Preheat the oven to 180°C (350°F).
2. Wrap sweet potatoes in foil and bake for 45-60 minutes.
3. Slice and serve warm.

Bamboo Shoot and Miso Stir-Fry

Ingredients:

- 1 cup bamboo shoots, sliced
- 1 tbsp miso paste
- 1 tbsp soy sauce
- 1 tbsp sesame oil
- 1 green onion, chopped

Instructions:

1. Heat sesame oil in a pan and sauté bamboo shoots for 3 minutes.
2. Stir in miso paste and soy sauce.
3. Cook for another 2 minutes and garnish with green onions.

Samurai Tea-Pickled Plums (Umeboshi)

Ingredients:

- 500g green ume plums
- 100g salt
- 1 cup shiso leaves
- 2 cups green tea (for soaking)

Instructions:

1. Soak plums in green tea overnight.
2. Drain and rub with salt.
3. Pack in a jar with shiso leaves and weigh down with a heavy object.
4. Ferment for at least 3 weeks before eating.

Grilled Venison with Salt and Miso

Ingredients:

- 300g venison steak
- 1 tbsp miso paste
- 1 tsp salt
- 1 tbsp sake
- 1 tbsp soy sauce

Instructions:

1. Marinate venison in miso, salt, sake, and soy sauce for 30 minutes.
2. Grill over charcoal or a hot pan for 3-4 minutes per side.
3. Let rest, slice, and serve.

Charred Rice Balls (Yaki Onigiri)

Ingredients:

- 2 cups cooked rice
- 1 tbsp soy sauce
- 1 tbsp miso paste
- 1 tbsp sesame oil

Instructions:

1. Shape rice into small balls or triangles.
2. Brush with a mix of soy sauce and miso paste.
3. Grill or pan-sear until crispy on both sides.
4. Serve warm.

Samurai-Style Fermented Soybeans (Natto)

Ingredients:

- 2 cups soybeans
- 1/4 tsp natto spores (Bacillus subtilis)
- 2 tbsp warm water

Instructions:

1. Soak soybeans overnight, then steam or boil until soft.
2. Dissolve natto spores in warm water and mix with the beans.
3. Spread beans in a shallow container and cover loosely with cheesecloth.
4. Incubate at 40°C (104°F) for 24-48 hours until sticky and aromatic.
5. Store in the fridge for a few days before eating.

Wild Mushroom and Tofu Soup

Ingredients:

- 4 cups dashi broth
- 1 cup assorted wild mushrooms (shiitake, maitake, enoki)
- 1/2 block firm tofu, cubed
- 1 tbsp miso paste
- 1 green onion, sliced

Instructions:

1. Heat dashi broth and add mushrooms. Simmer for 5 minutes.
2. Stir in miso paste and tofu, then cook for another 3 minutes.
3. Serve with sliced green onions on top.

Smoked Fish with Wasabi Leaves

Ingredients:

- 2 fillets of fish (mackerel, salmon, or trout)
- 1 tbsp salt
- 1 tbsp sake
- 1/2 cup wasabi leaves, chopped
- 1 cup wood chips (for smoking)

Instructions:

1. Rub fish with salt and sake, then let sit for 30 minutes.
2. Rinse and pat dry.
3. Smoke over wood chips for 15-20 minutes.
4. Serve with chopped wasabi leaves on top.

Samurai Hot Pot with Mountain Herbs

Ingredients:

- 4 cups dashi broth
- 200g thinly sliced venison or wild boar
- 1 cup mountain herbs (mizuna, wild mustard greens, shiso)
- 1/2 block firm tofu, sliced
- 1 tbsp soy sauce
- 1 tbsp miso paste

Instructions:

1. Heat dashi broth in a pot and add miso paste and soy sauce.
2. Add venison slices and cook until tender.
3. Add tofu and mountain herbs, simmer for another 5 minutes.
4. Serve hot.

Salted and Dried Fish (Himono)

Ingredients:

- 2 whole small fish (horse mackerel, sardines, or flounder)
- 1/4 cup salt
- 2 cups water

Instructions:

1. Dissolve salt in water and soak fish for 1-2 hours.
2. Remove, rinse, and pat dry.
3. Hang in a cool, airy place for 1-2 days until fully dried.
4. Grill or pan-fry before eating.

Burdock Root and Carrot Stir-Fry (Kinpira Gobo)

Ingredients:

- 1 burdock root, julienned
- 1 carrot, julienned
- 1 tbsp soy sauce
- 1 tbsp mirin
- 1 tsp sesame oil
- 1 tsp toasted sesame seeds

Instructions:

1. Soak burdock root in water for 10 minutes to remove bitterness.
2. Heat sesame oil in a pan and sauté burdock and carrot.
3. Add soy sauce and mirin, stir-fry for 3 minutes.
4. Sprinkle with sesame seeds before serving.

Samurai Roasted Barley Tea (Mugicha)

Ingredients:

- 1/2 cup barley
- 4 cups water

Instructions:

1. Dry-roast barley in a pan until golden brown and fragrant.
2. Boil water and add roasted barley. Simmer for 10 minutes.
3. Strain and serve hot or chilled.

Rice with Chestnuts (Kuri Gohan)

Ingredients:

- 2 cups rice
- 10 chestnuts, peeled and chopped
- 2 cups water
- 1/2 tsp salt

Instructions:

1. Rinse rice and soak for 30 minutes.
2. Add chestnuts, water, and salt.
3. Cook as usual in a rice cooker or pot.
4. Let sit for 10 minutes before serving.

Fire-Grilled Wild Duck (Kamo Yaki)

Ingredients:

- 1 wild duck breast
- 1 tbsp salt
- 1 tbsp sake
- 1 tsp soy sauce

Instructions:

1. Score the duck skin and season with salt, sake, and soy sauce.
2. Grill over open flame or high heat for 5 minutes per side.
3. Let rest before slicing and serving.

Homemade Soy Sauce Pickles

Ingredients:

- 1 cucumber, sliced
- 1 daikon radish, sliced
- 1/2 cup soy sauce
- 1 tbsp mirin
- 1 tbsp sugar

Instructions:

1. Mix soy sauce, mirin, and sugar in a jar.
2. Add sliced vegetables and submerge completely.
3. Refrigerate for at least 12 hours before eating.

Sake-Marinated Salmon (Saikyo Yaki)

Ingredients:

- 2 salmon fillets
- 2 tbsp white miso
- 2 tbsp sake
- 1 tbsp mirin
- 1 tbsp sugar

Instructions:

1. Mix miso, sake, mirin, and sugar into a paste.
2. Coat salmon fillets and marinate for 24 hours.
3. Grill or broil for 5-7 minutes per side.

Dried Tofu (Koya Dofu) in Miso Broth

Ingredients:

- 4 pieces dried tofu (Koya Dofu)
- 4 cups dashi broth
- 2 tbsp miso paste
- 1 tbsp soy sauce
- 1 tsp mirin
- 1 green onion, sliced

Instructions:

1. Soak dried tofu in warm water for 10 minutes, then gently squeeze out excess water.
2. Heat dashi broth and add miso paste, soy sauce, and mirin.
3. Add tofu and simmer for 5 minutes.
4. Garnish with sliced green onions before serving.

Wild Greens and Sesame Dressing (Gomaae)

Ingredients:

- 2 cups mixed wild greens (mustard greens, mizuna, or wild spinach)
- 2 tbsp toasted sesame seeds
- 1 tbsp soy sauce
- 1 tsp mirin
- 1 tsp sugar

Instructions:

1. Blanch wild greens in boiling water for 30 seconds, then drain and cool.
2. Grind sesame seeds and mix with soy sauce, mirin, and sugar.
3. Toss greens in the sesame dressing before serving.

Fermented Radish and Daikon Salad

Ingredients:

- 1 cup thinly sliced radish
- 1 cup thinly sliced daikon
- 1/2 tsp salt
- 1 tbsp rice vinegar
- 1 tsp soy sauce

Instructions:

1. Sprinkle salt over radish and daikon slices, then let sit for 30 minutes.
2. Rinse and squeeze out excess moisture.
3. Toss with rice vinegar and soy sauce before serving.

Boiled Lotus Root with Miso Glaze

Ingredients:

- 1 lotus root, peeled and sliced
- 2 cups water
- 1 tbsp miso paste
- 1 tbsp soy sauce
- 1 tsp mirin

Instructions:

1. Boil lotus root slices in water for 5 minutes, then drain.
2. In a pan, mix miso, soy sauce, and mirin, then heat gently.
3. Add lotus root slices and coat with the glaze before serving.

Lightly Salted Cucumber and Wakame Salad

Ingredients:

- 1 cucumber, thinly sliced
- 1/4 cup dried wakame seaweed
- 1/2 tsp salt
- 1 tbsp rice vinegar
- 1 tsp soy sauce

Instructions:

1. Sprinkle salt over cucumbers and let sit for 10 minutes, then rinse.
2. Soak wakame in water for 5 minutes, then drain.
3. Toss cucumber and wakame with rice vinegar and soy sauce.

Grilled Tofu with Miso Sauce

Ingredients:

- 1 block firm tofu, sliced into 1-inch pieces
- 2 tbsp miso paste
- 1 tbsp mirin
- 1 tbsp soy sauce
- 1 tsp sugar

Instructions:

1. Grill tofu pieces until golden brown on both sides.
2. Mix miso, mirin, soy sauce, and sugar, then spread over the tofu.
3. Grill for another 1-2 minutes until miso caramelizes.

Samurai-Style Herbal Tea Blend

Ingredients:

- 1 tbsp dried mugwort
- 1 tbsp dried shiso leaves
- 1 tbsp roasted barley
- 4 cups boiling water

Instructions:

1. Combine all dried herbs in a teapot.
2. Pour boiling water over them and steep for 5-7 minutes.
3. Strain and serve hot.

Barley Rice with Mountain Vegetables

Ingredients:

- 1 cup white rice
- 1/2 cup barley
- 2 cups water
- 1/2 cup mountain vegetables (fiddleheads, wild greens, bamboo shoots)
- 1/2 tsp salt

Instructions:

1. Rinse rice and barley, then soak for 30 minutes.
2. Add water, salt, and mountain vegetables.
3. Cook as usual in a rice cooker or on the stovetop.

Wild Ginger Rice Porridge

Ingredients:

- 1/2 cup rice
- 4 cups water
- 1 tbsp grated wild ginger
- 1/2 tsp salt
- 1 green onion, sliced

Instructions:

1. Cook rice and water in a pot over low heat until thick and creamy.
2. Stir in grated wild ginger and salt.
3. Serve with sliced green onions on top.

Dried Squid with Vinegar and Miso

Ingredients:

- 1 dried squid, cut into strips
- 2 tbsp rice vinegar
- 1 tbsp miso paste
- 1 tsp sugar

Instructions:

1. Lightly grill or toast dried squid until fragrant.
2. Mix rice vinegar, miso, and sugar.
3. Dip squid pieces into the sauce before eating.

Soy Sauce-Braised Bamboo Shoots

Ingredients:

- 1 cup bamboo shoots, sliced
- 2 tbsp soy sauce
- 1 tbsp mirin
- 1 tsp sugar
- 1/2 cup water

Instructions:

1. Combine soy sauce, mirin, sugar, and water in a pan.
2. Add bamboo shoots and simmer for 10 minutes.
3. Serve warm as a side dish.

Hand-Pulled Udon Noodles

Ingredients:

- 2 cups all-purpose flour
- ½ cup water
- ½ tsp salt
- Cornstarch (for dusting)

Instructions:

1. Dissolve salt in water. Gradually mix it into the flour until a dough forms.
2. Knead for 10-15 minutes until smooth, then wrap and let rest for 1 hour.
3. Roll out dough and cut into thin strips.
4. Boil in salted water for 7-8 minutes, then drain and rinse with cold water.
5. Serve with dashi broth or soy-based dipping sauce.

Mountain Yam Grated Over Rice (Tororo Gohan)

Ingredients:

- 1 small mountain yam (nagaimo)
- 1 cup steamed rice
- 1 tsp soy sauce
- 1 tsp dashi broth
- 1/2 tsp wasabi (optional)

Instructions:

1. Peel and grate the mountain yam into a sticky paste.
2. Mix with soy sauce and dashi broth.
3. Pour over warm steamed rice and top with wasabi if desired.

Black Sesame Rice Balls

Ingredients:

- 2 cups cooked sushi rice
- 2 tbsp black sesame seeds
- 1/2 tsp salt
- 1 sheet nori (optional)

Instructions:

1. Lightly toast black sesame seeds in a pan.
2. Mix sesame seeds and salt into warm rice.
3. Shape into small balls or triangular onigiri.
4. Wrap with nori if desired.

Wild Mushroom and Wild Rice Pilaf

Ingredients:

- 1 cup wild rice
- 2 cups water or dashi broth
- 1 cup mixed wild mushrooms (shiitake, maitake, enoki)
- 1 tbsp soy sauce
- 1 tsp mirin
- 1/2 tsp salt

Instructions:

1. Rinse wild rice and soak for 30 minutes.
2. Sauté mushrooms in a pan until fragrant.
3. Add rice, soy sauce, mirin, salt, and broth.
4. Simmer until rice is tender (about 40 minutes).

Soba Noodles in Hot Dashi Broth

Ingredients:

- 2 servings soba noodles
- 4 cups dashi broth
- 1 tbsp soy sauce
- 1 tbsp mirin
- 1 green onion, sliced

Instructions:

1. Cook soba noodles according to package instructions, then rinse with cold water.
2. Heat dashi broth with soy sauce and mirin.
3. Serve noodles in the hot broth, topped with green onions.

Slow-Simmered Wild Boar and Root Vegetables

Ingredients:

- 1 lb wild boar meat, cubed
- 1 carrot, sliced
- 1 daikon radish, sliced
- 4 cups dashi broth
- 2 tbsp miso paste
- 1 tbsp soy sauce

Instructions:

1. Sear wild boar meat in a pot.
2. Add dashi broth and simmer for 1 hour.
3. Add carrots and daikon, cook until tender.
4. Stir in miso paste and soy sauce before serving.

Samurai Green Tea Rice (Ochazuke)

Ingredients:

- 1 cup steamed rice
- ½ cup hot green tea or dashi broth
- 1 tsp soy sauce
- 1 sheet nori, shredded
- 1 tsp toasted sesame seeds

Instructions:

1. Place warm rice in a bowl.
2. Pour hot green tea or dashi broth over the rice.
3. Sprinkle with soy sauce, nori, and sesame seeds.

Fire-Grilled Salmon with Yuzu Citrus

Ingredients:

- 2 salmon fillets
- 1 tbsp yuzu juice
- 1 tsp soy sauce
- 1/2 tsp salt
- 1/2 tsp grated ginger

Instructions:

1. Marinate salmon with yuzu juice, soy sauce, salt, and ginger for 30 minutes.
2. Grill over an open flame until crispy and golden.
3. Serve hot with a side of rice.

www.ingramcontent.com/pod-product-compliance
Lightning Source LLC
LaVergne TN
LVHW081502060526
838201LV00056BA/2891